The Clink Clank Clunk

Written by
Jill Atkins

Illustrated by
Daniel Duncan

Frank Jenkins had a shed.

He filled it with junk.

He had planks of wood and a metal tank.

He had lots of tin cans, an oil drum, some string and some wire.

He had a horn that honked and a chain with fifteen links.

On Sunday, Frank's grandchildren came to the shed.

"What shall I do with all this junk?" Frank asked them.

"Make something we can play with," said Errol.

"Yes," said Jessica. "So we can have lots of fun."

Frank Jenkins got out his hammer, spanner and wire cutters. He had nails, screws and some wire.

"Right," he said with a wink. "Come back next Saturday."

"Thank you!" said Errol and Jessica.

On Monday, Frank took some nails and hammered the planks to six tin cans.

He made a lot of loud sounds!

Bang! Bang! Bang!

On Tuesday, Frank tied the planks to the oil drum with the wire.

He cut the wire with the wire cutters.

Snip! Snip! Snip!

On Wednesday, Frank stuck the tank to the planks with fifteen screws.

Then he checked that they were fixed well.

Squeak! Squeak! Squeak!

On Thursday, Frank tied the horn to the tank with string.

He sounded the horn. **Honk! Honk! Honk!**

"I hope Errol and Jessica like it," he said to himself.

On Friday, Frank fixed the chain with its fifteen links.

Clink! Clink! Clink!

"Now it's finished," said Frank with a smile. "**And** I'm getting rid of a lot of junk!"

On Saturday morning, Errol and Jessica came back.

"We can't wait to see what you have made, Grandad," said Jessica.

"I hope it will be fun," said Errol, as they went to the shed.

When the children saw what Frank had made, they hugged him.

"Oh, Grandad!" cried Jessica. "This looks fantastic! But … what is it?"

"I think I'll name it the Clink Clank Clunk," said Frank.

"Can we test it out?" shouted Errol.

"We'll go to the pond," said Frank Jenkins. "It's not deep."

"Will it float?" asked Errol.

"I think so," said Frank.

They reached the bank and slid the Clink Clank Clunk onto the pond.

Then they slipped their lifejackets on.

"Look!" shouted Jessica. "It didn't sink!"

They clambered onto the Clink Clank Clunk and still it didn't sink.

Did they have fun? Yes, they did!

"Thank you, Grandad," said Jessica. "You made us a terrific present from all that junk."

Frank Jenkins grinned.

"Now I'll have to start collecting junk again," he said. "I need something to fill my shed!"